I SPY
Thanksgiving Book
For Kids Ages 4-6

This Book Belongs to

_____

Fun Hint

All the pages can be colored in for extra fun!

I SPY with my little eye something starting with the letter

I SPY with my little eye something starting with the letter

I SPY with my little eye something starting with the letter

I SPY with my little eye something starting with the letter

I SPY with my little eye something starting with the letter

I SPY with my little eye something starting with the letter

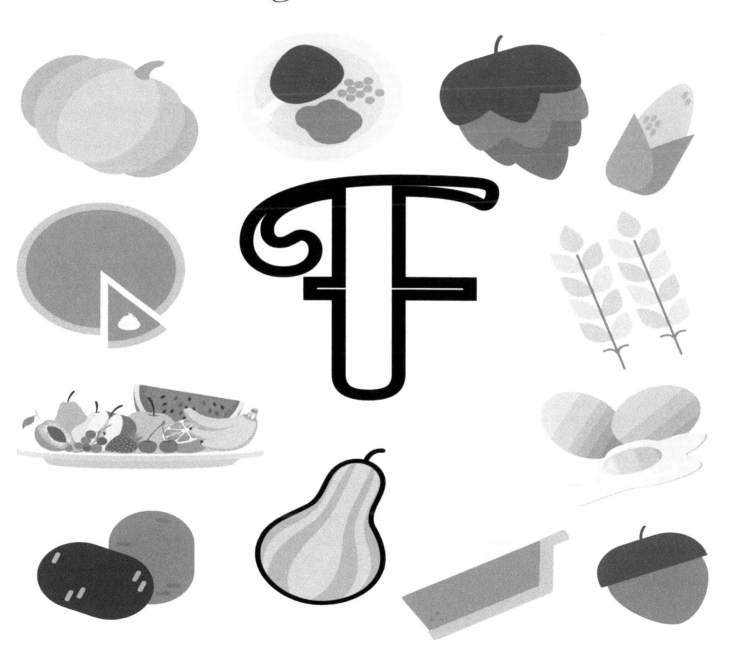

I SPY with my little eye something starting with the letter

I SPY with my little eye something starting with the letter

I SPY with my little eye something starting with the letter

I SPY with my little eye something starting with the letter

I SPY with my little eye something starting with the letter

I SPY with my little eye something starting with the letter

I SPY with my little eye something starting with the letter

I SPY with my little eye something starting with the letter

I SPY with my little eye something starting with the letter

I SPY with my little eye something starting with the letter

I SPY with my little eye something starting with the letter

I SPY with my little eye something starting with the letter

I SPY with my little eye something starting with the letter

I SPY with my little eye something starting with the letter

I SPY with my little eye something starting with the letter

I SPY with my little eye something starting with the letter

I SPY with my little eye something starting with the letter

I SPY with my little eye something starting with the letter

I SPY with my little eye something starting with the letter

I SPY with my little eye something starting with the letter

Congratulations on getting through the alphabet!

If you enjoyed this activity book, please leave a review and let us know what you liked the most!

You can find the all the I Spy answers at the back!

As a thank you for purchasing this book, enjoy these bonus coloring pages from one of our coloring books!

A is for
Apple pie

B is for
Bread

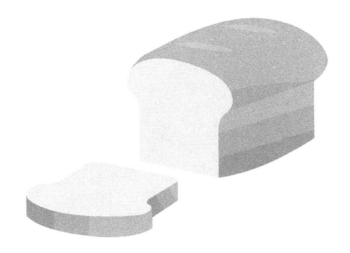

C is for
Corn

D is for Donut

E is for

Egg

F is for Fruits

G is for
Grapes

H is for
Home

I is for
Ice cream

J is for

Jar

K is for
Kiwi

L is for
Leaf

M is for
Maple Leaf

N is for
Nuts

O is for

Oven

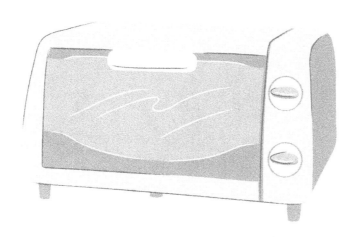

P is for Pumpkin

Q is for

Queen

R is for
Rose

S is for
Sunflower

T is for Turkey

U is for
Unicorn

V is for Vegetable

W is for
Wheat

X is for

Xylophone

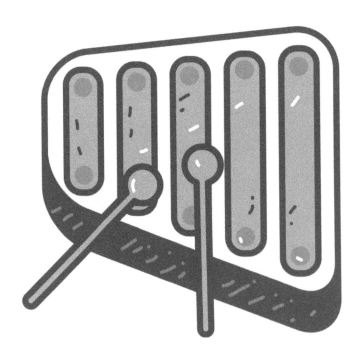

Y is for
Yam

Z is for
Zebra

Happy Thanksgiving!

A Message From the Publisher

Hello! My name is Harper and I am the owner of Happy Harper Publishing, the publishing house that brought you this title.

My hope is that your little one loved this book and enjoyed each and every page. If they did, please think about leaving a review for us on Amazon or wherever you purchased this book. It may only take a moment, but it really does mean the world for small businesses like mine.

The mission of Happy Harper is to create premium content for children that will help them learn new things, grow their imaginations, improve their motor skills, and have lots of fun doing it. Without you, however, this would not be possible, so we sincerely thank you for your purchase and for supporting our company mission.

~ Harper

Check out our other books!

For more, visit our Amazon store at:
amazon.com/author/happyharper

CPSIA information can be obtained
at www.ICGtesting.com
Printed in the USA
LVHW101044261020
669801LV00001B/100

9 781989 968536